11/02

Please visit our web site at: **www.garethstevens.com**
For a free color catalog describing Gareth Stevens Publishing's list of high-quality books and multimedia programs, call 1-800-542-2595 or fax your request to (414) 332-3567.

Library of Congress Cataloging-in-Publication Data

Whittaker, Nicola.
    [Creature feet]
    Feet / by Nicola Whittaker.
      p. cm. — (Creature features)
    Includes index.
    Summary: Simple text and photographs show different kinds of feet and various things they can do. Includes a picture glossary which identifies the animals pictured and provides information to help with classification skills.
    ISBN 0-8368-3163-2 (lib. bdg.)
    1. Foot—Juvenile literature. [1. Foot.] I. Title.
QL950.7.W45   2002
591.47'9—dc21   2002019531

This North American edition first published in 2002 by
Gareth Stevens Publishing
A World Almanac Education Group Company
330 West Olive Street, Suite 100
Milwaukee, Wisconsin 53212 USA

This U.S. edition © 2002 by Gareth Stevens, Inc. Original edition © 2001 by Franklin Watts.
First published in 2001 by Franklin Watts, 96 Leonard Street, London WC2A 4XD, England.

Franklin Watts editor: Samantha Armstrong
Franklin Watts designer: Jason Anscomb
Science consultant: Dr. Jim Flegg

Gareth Stevens editor: Dorothy L. Gibbs
Cover design: Tammy Gruenewald

Picture credits:
NHPA: 4 and cover (Eero Murtomaki), 5 and cover (Martin Harvey), 6-7 (A.N.T.),
8-9 (Joe Blossom), 10-11 (John Shaw), 14-15 (Karl Switak), 16-17 (N. A. Callow),
18-19 (Daniel Heuclin), 22 (Stephen Dalton), 23 (Manfred Danegger), 24 (E. A. Janes).
Oxford Scientific Films: 12 (Mickey Gibson), 20 (J. and P. Wegner).
Planet Earth Pictures: 13 (Peter J. Oxford), 21 (Jonathan Scott).
Simon Russell: 25.
Franklin Watts Photo Library: 26-27.

Printed in Hong Kong

1 2 3 4 5 6 7 8 9 06 05 04 03 02

FEET

Written by
Nicola Whittaker

Gareth Stevens Publishing
A WORLD ALMANAC EDUCATION GROUP COMPANY

Different
creatures have

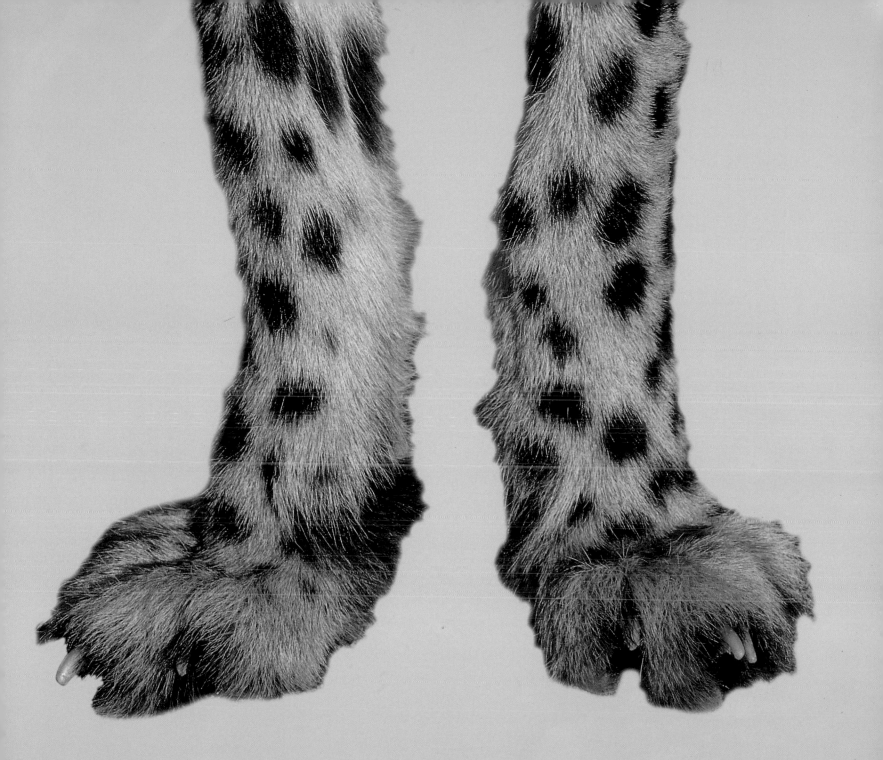

different **feet**.

Some have **flippers**.

some have
paws.

Some have **toes**.

Some have

claws!

Some
have two
feet.

13

Some have

four.

Some have
eight **feet**.

17

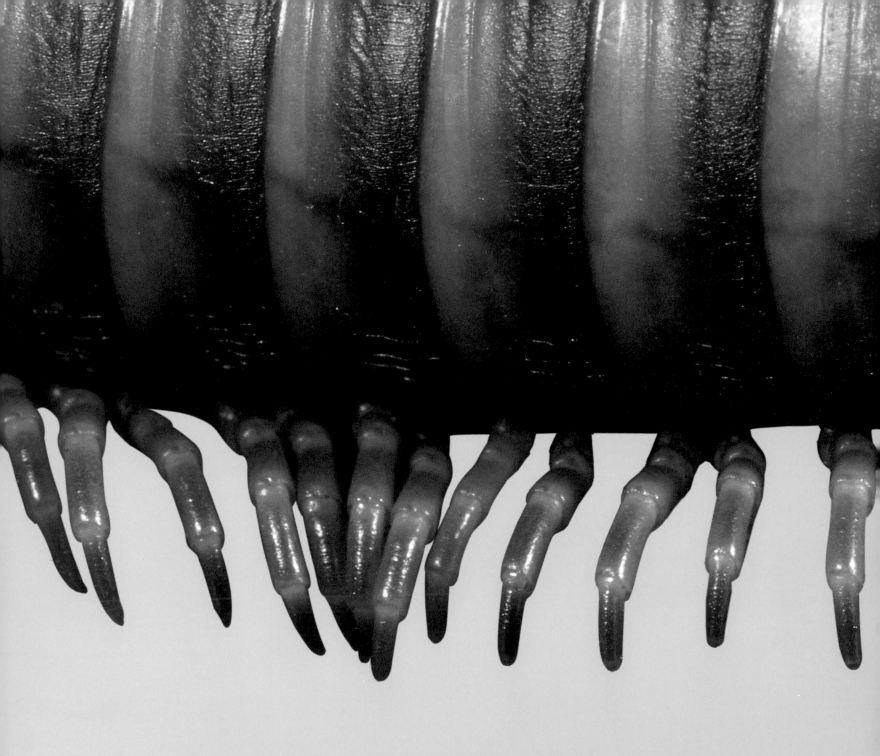

Some have

more!

some feet
are

small.

some feet
are **big**.

Some feet can

hop.

Some feet
can **dig**.

Some have **socks**.

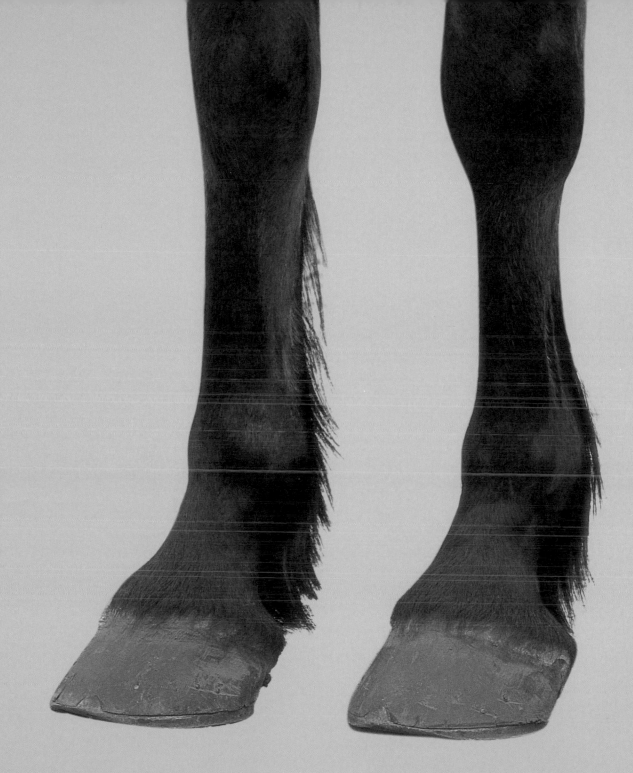

Some wear a **shoe**.

But I like **my** feet!

How about **you**?

Featured

White-tailed Eagle
Bird (hawk/eagle family)
Lives: Europe
Eats: fish
Snatches fish from the water with its sharp claws, or talons.

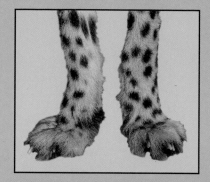

Cheetah
Mammal (cat family)
Lives: African plains
Eats: birds and small mammals
Can run faster than any other land animal in the world.

New Zealand Fur Seal
Mammal (seal/sea lion family)
Lives: Pacific Ocean
Eats: fish
Thick, waterproof fur keeps its skin dry, even in the ocean.

Polar Bear
Mammal (bear family)
Lives: northern polar regions
Eats: seals, fish, and birds
Thick fur protects it from the icy cold.

Creatures

Koala
Mammal (marsupial family)
Lives: Australian woodland
Eats: eucalyptus leaves
Sleeps all day and spends most
of its time in treetops.

Land Crab
Crustacean (crab family)
Lives: tropical beaches
Eats: mostly plants
Can move in any direction,
including sideways.

Greater Flamingo
Bird (flamingo family)
Lives: shallow, salty lakes
Eats: fish and water insects
Has long, thin legs with knees
that seem to bend backward.

Yellow Fan-Fingered Gecko
Reptile (lizard family)
Lives: North Africa
Eats: insects
Sticky pads on its feet grip smooth
surfaces, even upside down.

Featured

Orb-Web Spider
Arachnid (spider family)
Lives: Europe
Eats: insects
Spins silk into a sticky web that traps insects for food.

Giant Millipede
Myriapod (centipede/millipede family)
Lives: South America
Eats: decaying plants
May have up to 300 legs.

Golden Hamster
Mammal (rat/mouse family)
Lives: Middle East
Eats: seeds and fruit
Now almost extinct in the wild in its homeland, Syria.

African Elephant
Mammal (elephant family)
Lives: Africa
Eats: plants
Is the largest land animal in the world.

Creatures

Tree Frog
Amphibian (frog family)
Lives: Europe
Eats: insects and spiders
Sticky toe pads help it cling
to leaves.

Mole
Mammal (mole family)
Lives: Europe
Eats: worms and insects
Uses its curved front feet and
long claws to dig tunnels.

Birman Seal Point Cat
Mammal (cat family)
Lives: worldwide
Eats: pet foods
Bred specially to be a pet and
for its pure white feet.

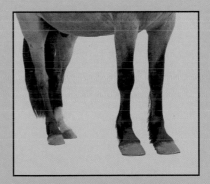

Horse
Mammal (horse family)
Lives: worldwide
Eats: grass
Its hooves are really nails
that cover its middle toes.

Index

(**Boldface** entries indicate pictures.)